SINNERS IN THE HANDS OF AN ANGRY GOD

by

JONATHAN EDWARDS

MADE EASIER TO READ

by

JOHN JEFFERY FANELLA

P&R
PUBLISHING

P.O. BOX 817 • PHILLIPSBURG • NEW JERSEY 08865-0817

Unless otherwise indicated, Scripture quotations are from The Holy Bible, New King James Version. Copyright © 1979, 1980, 1982, Thomas Nelson, Inc.

Printed in the United States of America

Library of Congress Cataloging-in-Publication Data

Fanella, John Jeffery, 1970
    Sinners in the hands of an angry God / by Jonathan Edwards ; made easier to read [by] John Jeffery Fanella.
        p.   cm.
    ISBN-10: 0-87552-213-0 (pbk.)
    ISBN-13: 978-0-87552-213-5 (pbk.)
    1. Evangelistic sermons. 2. Congregational churches—Sermons. 3. Sermons, American. I. Edwards, Jonathan, 1703–1758. Sinners in the hands of an angry God. II. Title.
BV3797.E38   1996
252'.3—dc20   96-22884

Foreword

ENFIELD, CONNECTICUT—July 8, 1741. Jonathan Edwards, a Massachusetts pastor, is the visiting preacher in a friend's pulpit for the evening service. On the previous night, the devout women of the community have prayed that God would demonstrate His power in the settlement. Edwards quietly rises to preach. His text is Deuteronomy 32:35–36: "To me belongeth vengeance, and recompense; their foot shall slide in due time: for the day of their calamity is at hand, and the things that shall come upon them make haste. For the LORD shall judge his people" (KJV). After announcing his theme, "Sinners in the Hands of an Angry God," Edwards preaches on the wrath of God in store for people who do not turn from their sin.

The response is remarkable. The language and imagery are so vivid that many in the congregation tremble uncontrollably, some cry out for mercy, and others faint. According to one reliable witness, there were "moanings and cryings, until the shrieks became so amazing that

3

Edwards (his eyes fixed on the bell-rope) had to pause" (Cited in Perry Miller, *Jonathan Edwards* [William Sloan Associates: New York, 1949], 145).

Edwards stood on solid biblical ground when he characterized God as an angry Judge. Scripture tells us, "God is a just judge, and God is angry with the wicked every day" (Ps. 7:11). Twentieth-century readers, however, accustomed to being spoon-fed nice homilies about God's benevolence, and having little understanding of His wrath, are often appalled by the terrifying picture Edwards painted of God. In fact (chiefly because of the notoriety of this sermon), Edwards has acquired the reputation of being a stern and loveless preacher who delighted in terrifying his hearers with colorful descriptions of the torments of hell.

But that is a totally false caricature. He was actually a warm and sensitive pastor, as well as a meticulous theologian. Those closest to him knew him as a gentle, loving husband, father, and friend, who gave generously to the poor and distressed.

Furthermore, Edwards was neither fiery nor manipulative. In fact, he read his message in a carefully controlled tone just so that his primary appeal would be to his hearers' *minds*, not their emotions. The force of his delivery lay not in his voice or gestures but in his lucid, powerful reasoning and intense conviction. Many consider him the greatest philosopher-theologian to have graced the American scene. Nevertheless, notes J. I. Packer, Edwards "studied plainness of style, concealing his learning beneath a deliberately bald clarity of statement (J. I. Packer, *A Quest for Godliness: The Puritan Vision of the Christian Life* [Wheaton, Ill.: Crossway Books, 1990], 313).

As evidence of Edwards's concern for his listeners, "Sinners in the Hands of an Angry God" ends with a tender gospel appeal. One man who was present that evening wrote in his diary,

> Several Souls were hopefully wrought upon [that] night. & oh ye cheerfulness and pleasantness of their countenances [that] receiv^d comfort—oh [that] God wd strengthen and confirm—we sung an hymn & pray^d & dismiss^d ye Assembly. (Cited in Iain H. Murray, *Jonathan Edwards: A New Biography* [Edinburgh: Banner of Truth, 1987], 169.)

In fact, five hundred people were converted in the community that day, sparking one of the most dramatic episodes of revival in the Great Awakening.

I AM GRATEFUL for this modern-language adaptation of Edwards's famous sermon. It is faithful in every regard to the original, unfolding for modern readers the graphic intensity of Edwards's majestic sermon on divine wrath. I know of no more powerful exposition of God's anger against sin than this landmark sermon by the most profound Christian mind America has ever seen. It contains a message that is sadly neglected today. But it is a *biblical* message, and worthy of our serious attention. My prayer is that it will stir many careless souls out of their stupor, and that it will encourage today's preachers to proclaim the whole counsel of God boldly.

JOHN F. MACARTHUR, JR.

Enfield, Connecticut
July 8, 1741

Deuteronomy 32:35
—*"Their foot shall slip in due time."*—

IN THIS VERSE the violent anger of God is threatened upon the wicked and unbelieving Israelites, who were God's chosen people living under the benefits of His grace, but who, despite all God's wonderful works toward them, were without sense and had no understanding in them (Deuteronomy 32:28). Though cultivated by the blessings of heaven, they brought forth only bitter and poisonous fruit (vv. 32–33). The verse I have chosen for my text, "Their foot shall slip in due time," relates to the punishment and destruction of these wicked Israelites. It implies the following things:

1. They were always exposed to destruction, just as someone who stands or walks in slippery places is always in danger of falling. The destruction of the Israel-

ites is implied in the text by their foot slipping. The same idea is expressed in Psalm 73:18: "Surely You set them in slippery places; You cast them down to destruction."

2. It also implies that they were always exposed to sudden, unexpected destruction. Just as he who walks in slippery places is always liable to fall, he cannot foresee from one moment to the next whether he will stand or fall. When he does fall, it is sudden and without warning. This is also expressed in Psalm 73:18–19: "Surely You set them in slippery places; You cast them down to destruction. Oh, how they are brought to desolation, as in a moment! They are utterly consumed with terrors."

3. Another thing this text implies is that they are capable of falling totally on their own; they do not have to be thrown down by another person. Like someone who stands or walks on slippery ground, they need only their own weight to make them fall.

4. The only reason they have not fallen already is that God's appointed time has not yet come. The text says that when their appointed time does come, "their foot shall slip." Then, by their own weight they will be left to fall. God will not hold them up in these slippery places any longer but will let them go; and at the very instant He does, they will fall into destruction. As a man standing on the slippery slope at the edge of a pit cannot stand unassisted, when he is let go, he immediately falls and is lost.

From these words I would insist on this: Nothing keeps wicked people out of hell for a single moment except the mere pleasure of God. By the mere pleasure of God I mean His *sovereign* pleasure, which is not hindered or restrained by anything. It is only the sovereign will of God that preserves the life of a wicked person. Nothing else preserves the wicked for one moment except God's mere will. The truth of this observation may be seen in the following thoughts:

1. God does not lack the power to throw wicked people into hell at any moment. The hands of man are weak when God rises up against him. The strongest of men are defenseless against God, and no one can be rescued from His hand.

God is not only *able* to throw people into hell, but He is also able to do it *easily*. Sometimes a ruler struggles to subdue a rebel because the rebel has strengthened his position and rallied other men to his aid. But this is not the way it is with God. Nothing can defend you from *His* power. Even though wicked people join in great numbers against Him, they are easily broken into pieces. They are like great piles of weightless chaff in a tornado, or large heaps of dry stubble in the path of devouring flames.

We find it easy to step on and crush a worm crawling on the ground, and it is easy for us to cut or burn a thin thread by which an object hangs. It is just as easy for God to cast His wicked enemies into hell whenever He pleases. Who are we to think that we can stand against Him whose rebuke makes the earth shake and the mountains fall?

2. The wicked deserve to be thrown into hell. God is not unjust in using His power to destroy them. No, on the contrary, justice calls aloud for an infinite punishment of their sins. Divine justice says of the tree that bears grapes like Sodom, "Cut it down; why does it use up the ground?" (Luke 13:7). The sword of divine jus-

tice waves over their heads at every moment, and nothing but God's sovereign mercy and mere will holds it from falling on them.

3. Wicked people are already under a sentence of condemnation to hell. Not only do they justly deserve to be thrown down into hell, but the sentence of God's eternal and unchangeable standard of righteousness (His law)—which He has placed between Himself and mankind, stands against them so that they are already hanging over hell. John 3:18 says, "He who does not believe is condemned already." This means that every unconverted person rightfully belongs to hell. That is his place, where he is from—"You are from beneath" (John 8:23)— and he is bound for hell. It is hell that God's justice, His Word, and the sentence of His unchangeable law assign to the unconverted.

4. Wicked and unbelieving people are, even now, the objects of the very same anger and wrath of God that are revealed in the torments of hell. The reason they are not thrown down into hell now is not that the sovereign God is not angry with them, as He is with the many miserable people who are already tormented in hell and bearing His fierce wrath. No, God is much angrier with unbelievers who are still here on earth—and, very likely, with many now in this congregation—than He is with many of those now in the flames of hell.

So the reason why God has not loosened His hand and cut them off is not that He is unaware of their wickedness or tolerates it. God is not like them, though they imagine Him to be. The wrath of God is burning against them; their damnation is not sleeping; the pit is prepared; the fire is already made; the furnace is hot and ready to receive them. The flames, even now, rage and glow. The shiny sword is sharpened and held over them. The pit has opened its mouth under them.

5. The Devil also stands ready to fall on the wicked and take them as his own the moment God allows. They belong to the Devil; he has their souls in his possession and under his rule. The demons are watching them and are always at hand. As greedy, hungry lions wait for the opportune time to devour their prey, so the demons stand waiting for the wicked. They expect to get them but are held back for the moment. If God were to withdraw His hand, which is what restrains the demons, they would at once attack their poor souls. The Devil himself is staring at them with his mouth wide open, and the mouth of hell waits to receive them. If God were to allow it, the wicked would quickly be swallowed up and lost.

6. Within the souls of wicked people, hellish desires reign. Were it not for God's restraints, those desires would kindle and flare up into hellfire. In the very nature of carnal men lies the basis for the torments of hell. These corrupt desires controlling and possessing them are the very seeds of hellfire. They are active and extremely violent. If it were not for God's restraining hand, they would soon fan out as widely as the corruption and hostility that fill the hearts of the condemned, and produce the same kind of torment in them.

Scripture compares the souls of the wicked to the troubled sea: "But the wicked are like the troubled sea, when it cannot rest, whose waters cast up mire and dirt" (Isaiah 57:20). For the time, God is restraining their wickedness by His almighty power just as He restrains the raging waters of the troubled sea when He says, "This far you may come, but no farther, and here your proud waves must stop" (Job 38:11). But again, if God were to withdraw His restraining power, it would take all of them away.

Sin is the ruin and misery of the soul; it is destructive by nature, and, if God were to leave it unrestrained, nothing else would be needed to make the soul perfectly miserable. The heart is extremely corrupt, and its fury knows no boundaries. Sin is like fire confined by God's restraints, but if let loose, it would set ablaze the whole course of nature. The heart of man is now a pit full of sin, and if it were not restrained, it would immediately turn the soul into a fiery oven or a furnace of fire and brimstone.

7. It is no security to wicked people for one moment that they are in no apparent danger of dying soon. It is no security for the natural man that he is now healthy or that he does not foresee how he might suddenly be taken by some accident, though his present circumstances pose no visible danger. The long and varied history of humanity disproves the assumption that we are not on the very brink of eternity itself, and that our very next step will not be into another world. The unseen and unexpected ways that people suddenly leave this world are too numerous to imagine.

The unconverted walk over the pit of hell on a rotten bridge, and there are countless places on that bridge that are too weak to bear their weight. These places go unseen. The arrows of death fly unnoticed at high noon; the sharpest eyes cannot spot them.

God has so many unfathomable ways of taking wicked people out of this world and sending them to hell that He does not need miracles or unnatural causes to do so. His ordinary providence alone is able to destroy the wicked at any moment. All the means by which sinners leave this world are under His control. Those means are so subject to His power and choosing, that it depends no less on His will if God uses them than if He does not.

8. Natural men's diligence and care to preserve their own lives, or the efforts of others to preserve them, do not give them security for one moment. Divine providence and universal experience prove that. There is clear evidence that men's own wisdom is no security for them from death. If it were, we should see some difference between the educated and shrewd people, and plain people, in regard to their being subject to early, unexpected death. But how is it really? "How does a wise man die? As the fool!" (Ecclesiastes 2:16).

9. All the schemes and efforts of the wicked to escape hell while they continue to reject Christ and remain wicked do not secure them from hell one moment. Almost every natural man that hears about hell deceives himself that he will escape it. He rests in his own false security, flattering himself with the good things he has done, is now doing, or intends to do. Every man plots how he will escape damnation and flatters himself, thinking that his plans are ingenious and that his schemes will not fail. He clearly hears that only a few will be saved, and that the greater part of humanity who have died before him have gone to hell. But, each one imagines that his plans to escape are better than theirs. He has no intention of going to that place of torment; he tells himself that he will carry out his plans with such care that they cannot fail.

These foolish people miserably trick only themselves with their own schemes. By putting confidence in their own wisdom and strength, they are only trusting a shadow. Most of those who until now have lived under the same means of grace are now dead and in hell. This is not because they were not as wise or did not plan for their escape as well as those who are alive today. If we could ask them one by one whether, when they were alive and heard of hell, they ever expected to suffer its misery, they would doubtless say, "No, I never intended to come here. I had other plans. I thought I could manage well and my scheme was sound. I intended to carry out all of my plans, but death took me by surprise. I wasn't looking for it at that time or in that way. It came like a thief in the night. Death outsmarted me. God's wrath was too quick for me. O my cursed foolishness! All this time I was flattering myself with empty dreams of what I would do later. And just when I was saying to myself, 'Peace and safety,' destruction overcame me."

10. God is not bound by any promises to keep any natural man out of hell for one moment. He has certainly made no promises of eternal life or of any deliverance from eternal death, except those given in the covenant of grace—the promises to us in Christ, in whom all the promises are "Yes" and "Amen" (2 Corinthians 1:20). But surely those who are not children of the covenant—who disbelieve all of the promises and disregard the Mediator of the covenant—they have no share in the promises of this covenant of grace.

Therefore, regardless of what people have imagined and pretended about promises made to natural men's earnest seeking and knocking, it is clear that whatever pains one takes in religion, whatever prayers he makes, unless he believes in Christ, God is under no obligation to keep him from eternal destruction for one moment.

So it is that natural men are held in the hand of God over the pit of hell. They deserve the fiery pit and are already sentenced to it. God is dreadfully provoked, and His anger is as great toward them as it is toward those suffering His fierce wrath even now. They have done nothing to appease or lessen God's anger, nor is He under any obligation or promise to hold them up for one moment.

The Devil is waiting for them; hell's mouth is open for them; the flames gather and flash around them, longing to take them and swallow them up. The fire trapped inside their own hearts is struggling to break out, and they have no hope of a mediator. Nothing within their reach can give them any security. In short, they have no refuge and nothing to grab hold of. The only thing that preserves them every moment is the mere arbitrary will and the uncovenanted, unobliged patience of an incensed God.

APPLICATION

THE PURPOSE of this terrifying subject is to wake up the unconverted people in this congregation. What you have heard is true of every one of you who do not believe and trust in Christ. That world of misery, that lake of burning brimstone, is spread right beneath you. There is the dreadful pit of the glowing flames of God's wrath; there is hell's wide-open mouth, and you have nothing to stand on or to grab on to, nothing between you and hell but the air. Only the power and mere pleasure of God holds you up.

You are probably unaware of this. You notice that you are being kept out of hell, but you do not see that it is God's hand keeping you out. Instead, you look at other things such as your good health, the way you take care of yourself, and the things you do to preserve your life. But in fact, these things are nothing. If God withdrew His hand, these things would no more keep you from falling than thin air holds up a person suspended in it.

Your own wickedness weighs you down like lead and is dragging you down toward hell with great weight and force. Again, if God would let you go, you would immediately sink, quickly descending and plunging into the bottomless gulf. All of your health and personal care, all of your best schemes, and all of your own righteousness would no better support you and keep you out of hell than a spider's web would stop a falling rock.

If not for the sovereign pleasure of God, even the earth would not put up with you another moment because you are nothing but a burden to it. The creation is groaning because of you. The creatures of the earth are unwillingly subject to your corruption. The sun does not want to shine on you and give you its light so that you can serve sin and Satan. The earth does not want to produce food so that you can satisfy your lusts. Nor does it want to be a stage on which you act out all of your wickedness. The air does not want to fill your lungs with life while you spend that life serving God's enemies. God's creation is good and was created for man's use in serving God, not for any other purpose. You, though, cause it to groan when you abuse it by making it serve purposes for which it was not designed. The world would spit you out if it were not for the sovereign hand of God who, though having cursed it, gives it hope.

The black clouds of God's wrath are hanging directly over your head. They are full of a dreadful storm with its loud thunder, and if it were not for the restraining hand of God, it would immediately burst upon you. For now, the sovereign pleasure of God holds back the rough winds; otherwise, they would come with fury and your destruction would come as a tornado, and you would be blown away like dry chaff.

The wrath of God is like great waters that are temporarily dammed up. They keep rising higher and higher until they find an outlet. The longer they have been dammed up, the more rapid and powerful will be their flow once they are let loose. It is true that judgment against your evil works has not been carried out yet. But in the meantime your guilt has been building up, and every day you are storing up for yourself more wrath.

The waters are constantly rising and gathering might, and nothing but the mere pleasure of God holds them back, though they are unwilling to be stopped and are pushing with great force to break free. If God were just to lift His hand from the floodgate, it would immediately fly open and the fiery floods of the fierceness and wrath of God would rush forward with unbelievable fury and would overtake you with unlimited power. Even if your strength were ten thousand times greater than what it is, in fact, if it were ten thousand times greater than the boldest and most powerful devil in all of hell, it would not be able to withstand or endure it.

The bow of God's wrath is bent and straining. The arrow is already set on the string, and justice aims it directly at your heart. It is nothing but the mere pleasure of God—an angry God—who is not restrained by any promise or obligation, that keeps that arrow from being drunk with your blood. This means that all of you whose hearts have never been changed by the power of the Holy Spirit, and who have never been born again and made new creatures, raised from being dead in sin to a new light and life—all of you are in the hands of an angry God.

Though you may have made many changes in your life, or had some religious experiences, or practiced religion in your family, your private life, or your church, it is only God's mere pleasure that keeps you from being swallowed up in everlasting destruction this very moment. However unconvinced you are now about the truth of what you are hearing, when you die you will be fully convinced of it. Others who were in your position now see that these things are true. For most of them destruction came suddenly, when they least expected it. They were saying, "Peace and safety," but now they see that the things they trusted to give them peace and safety were nothing but thin air and empty shadows.

God is holding you over the pit of hell, as someone who holds a spider or some repulsive insect over a fire, and He abhors you and is dreadfully provoked. His wrath toward you burns like fire, and He sees you as worthy of nothing else but to be thrown into that fire. His eyes are too pure even to look at you; you are ten thousand times more detestable in His sight than the most hated poisonous snake is in ours. You have offended Him infinitely more than even a stubborn rebel did his prince. Yet, it is nothing but God's hand that holds you from falling into the fire every moment.

This is the only reason why you did not go to hell last night but were patiently allowed to wake up to this world again after you closed your eyes to sleep. It is also the reason why you have not dropped into hell since you woke up this morning. There can be no other reason given why you have not gone to hell even while sitting here in this church provoking His pure eyes by your sinful, wicked manner of participating in His sacred worship. I declare to you, there can be no other reason given why you do not fall into hell this very moment!

O sinner! Think seriously about the fearful danger you are in. God is holding you over a great furnace of wrath, a wide and bottomless pit full of the fire of His wrath. His wrath is provoked and enraged by you as much as it is against the many people who are already damned in hell. You are hanging by a slender thread with the flames of divine wrath burning around it, and they are ready to singe it and burn all the way through at any moment. Yet, you have no interest in a mediator, and nothing to grab hold of to save yourself, nothing to fend off the flames of wrath, nothing in yourself, nothing you have ever done, nothing you can do to persuade God to spare you for one moment. Consider here more specifically:

1. *Whose wrath it is. It is the wrath of the infinite God.* If it were only the wrath of man, even the wrath of the strongest prince, it would not compare with God's. People dread the wrath of kings, especially of dictators, who have people's lives and possessions totally under their power and can dispose of them at their mere will. Proverbs 20:2 says, "The wrath of a king is like the roaring of a lion; whoever provokes him to anger sins against his own life." An individual who greatly enrages a tyrannical prince will probably suffer the most extreme torments that human beings can invent or inflict. Yet

the greatest earthly rulers in all their majesty and strength when displaying their greatest terrors are but feeble, despicable worms of the dust in comparison with the great and almighty Creator and King of heaven and earth. They accomplish very little, even when they are greatly enraged and have exhibited the fullness of their fury.

All the kings of the earth are like grasshoppers before God. They are nothing, and even less than nothing. Both their love and their hatred are to be despised. The wrath of the great King of kings is much more terrible than theirs, just as His majesty is greater as well. Luke 12:4–5 says, "I say to you, My friends, do not be afraid of those who kill the body, and after that have no more that they can do. But I will show you whom you should fear: Fear Him who, after He has killed [the body], has power to cast [you] into hell; yes, I say to you, fear Him!"

2. *The fierceness of His wrath is what you are subject to.* We often read of the fury of God, as in Isaiah 59:18: "According to their deeds, accordingly He will repay, fury to His adversaries, recompense [retribution] to His enemies; the coastlands He will fully repay." Likewise Isaiah 66:16 says, "For by fire and by His sword the LORD will judge all flesh [all people]; and the slain of the LORD shall be many." Also, in many other places such as Revelation 19:15, we read, "He Himself treads the winepress of the fierceness and wrath of Almighty God." These words are extremely terrible. If the verse had only said, "the wrath of God," the words would have spoken of something infinitely dreadful. But it says, "the *fierceness* and wrath." It is the *fury* of God, the *fierceness* of Jehovah! Oh, how dreadful that must be! Who can speak or

think about what such expressions imply? Moreover, it is "the fierceness and wrath of *Almighty* God," as if to emphasize a great display of His almighty power in what His fierce wrath inflicts. As men are in the habit of showing their strength through the fierceness of their wrath, God's unlimited power is enraged and put into action. Oh, what will be the consequence then? What will happen to the poor worm who shall suffer His wrath? Whose hands are strong enough and whose heart can bear the pain? What a dreadful, inexpressible, and inconceivable depth of misery the poor creature will sink to who shall be the object of this wrath!

For those present here who remain unconverted, consider this: When the verse says that God will carry out the fierceness of His anger, it means that He will inflict His wrath without any pity. When God observes your indescribable punishment and sees your extreme torment to be far more than your strength can bear and that it is crushing you and making you sink into infinite gloom, He will have no compassion on you. He will not refrain from carrying out His wrath or lighten His hand in the least. There shall be no moderation or mercy, nor will God hold back His rough wind. He will have no regard for your welfare, nor will He be the least bit careful that you do not suffer too much, except that you do not suffer beyond what justice requires. Nothing will be withheld because it is too hard for you to bear. Ezekiel 8:18 says, "Therefore I also will act in fury. My eye will not spare nor will I have pity; and though they cry in My ears with a loud voice, I will not hear them."

For now, God stands ready to have pity on you; this is a day of mercy. Now you may cry with the hope of obtaining mercy. But once the day of mercy is past, your most serious and desperate cries for mercy will be in vain. You will be forever lost, and God will throw you away, no longer giving thought to your welfare. God will have no other use for you except to make you suffer misery; you shall exist for no other purpose. You will be objects of His wrath, "prepared for destruction" (Romans 9:22), and there will be no other use for those objects but to be filled full of God's wrath. God will be so far from pitying you when you cry to him, that the Bible says, He will only "laugh" and "mock" (Proverbs 1:26).

How awful are the words of the great God in Isaiah 63:3, "For I have trodden them in My anger, and trampled them in My fury; their blood is sprinkled upon My garments, and I have stained all My robes"! It is perhaps impossible to find words that express more vividly the ideas of contempt, hatred, and fierce anger. If you cry to God for pity, He will be far from pitying you in your sad state of showing you the least favor. Instead, He will only trample you under His feet. Although He will know that you cannot bear the weight of His unlimited power treading on you, He will not think twice but will still crush you under His feet without mercy. He will crush you until your blood splatters, sprinkling His garments and staining all of His clothes. Not only will He hate you, but He will hold you in the highest contempt. The only place fit for you will be under His feet to be stomped on like the filthy mud in the streets.

3. *The misery you will be exposed to will be for the purpose of showing what the wrath of God is.* God has wanted to show men and angels both how great His love is and how terrible His wrath is. Sometimes when kings want to display the extent of their wrath, they do so by severely punishing those who provoke them.

Nebuchadnezzar, that mighty and arrogant king of the Chaldean Empire, was willing to show his wrath when he was angered by Shadrach, Meshach, and Abednego. He gave the order to heat the fiery furnace seven times hotter than it was before. It was probably raised to the hottest degree man was capable of producing. In the same way, the great God is also willing to show *His* wrath and magnify *His* awesome majesty and mighty power in the extreme sufferings of His enemies. Romans 9:22 says, "What if God, wanting to show His wrath and to make His power known, endured with much longsuffering the vessels of wrath prepared for destruction . . . ?" Even more, because this display of His unrestrained wrath, fury, and fierceness is part of His plan, we know He will do it to its fullest degree.

What will be accomplished and brought to pass will be dreadful to witness. When the great and angry God has risen up and executed His terrifying vengeance on the poor sinner, and the wretch is actually suffering the infinite weight and power of His anger, then God will call upon the whole universe to behold the awful majesty and mighty power displayed in it. Isaiah 33:12–14 says, "'The people shall be like the burnings of lime; like thorns cut up they shall be burned in the fire. Hear, you who are afar off, what I have done; and you who are near, acknowledge My might.' The sinners in Zion are afraid; fearfulness has seized the hypocrites: 'Who among us shall dwell with the devouring fire? Who among us shall dwell with everlasting burnings?'"

This is how it will be for you who are unconverted if you continue in your unbelief. The infinite might, majesty, and terribleness of the all-powerful God shall be magnified on you in the inexpressible severity of your torment. You shall be tormented in the presence of the holy angels and also in the presence of the Lamb (Jesus Christ).

While you are in this state of suffering, the blessed inhabitants of heaven will go and look upon the dreadful sight so that they may see what the wrath and fierceness of the Almighty is. When they see it, they will fall down and adore such great power and majesty. Isaiah 66:23–24 says, "'From one New Moon to another, and from one Sabbath to another, all [people] shall come to worship before Me,' says the LORD. 'And they shall go forth and look upon the corpses of the men who have transgressed against Me. For their worm does not die, and their fire is not quenched. They shall be an abhorrence to all [people].'"

4. *It is an everlasting wrath.* It would be dreadful to suffer this fierceness and wrath of almighty God for even one moment, but you will suffer it for all eternity. There will be no end to this intense and horrible misery. When you look ahead you will see a long forever, an unlimited length of time before you. This will swallow up all of your thoughts. It will amaze your soul, and you will be in absolute despair of ever being delivered, of its ever coming to an end, or of receiving any reduction of torment or any rest at all. You will know for sure that you must wear out many long ages, millions and millions of ages, in struggling and fighting against this merciless vengeance. When you have struggled and fought through all of these many ages, you will realize that hardly a second has gone by and eternity still remains. Your punishment will be infinite. Oh, who can express the horrible state of a soul in that condition! All that we can possibly say about it is only a very feeble and

faint image of what it will be like. It is inexpressible and inconceivable, for "who knows the power of God's anger?"

How dreadful is the state of those who are in danger of this great wrath and infinite misery every hour of every day! Yet, this is the dark and gloomy condition of every soul in this congregation who has not been born again, however moral and strict, serious and religious he or she may be. Oh! that you would consider this, whether you are young or old!

There is reason to think that many in this congregation now listening to this message will actually suffer this very misery for all eternity. We do not know who they are or where they are seated or what they may now be thinking. It could be that they are now at ease and remain undisturbed by hearing all these things, assuring themselves that they are not the ones spoken of, and promising themselves that they will escape. If we knew that there was even one person in this whole congregation who would suffer such misery, what an awful thing it would be to think of! Even more, if we knew who that person was, how horrifying it would be to see the person in such a state! All the rest of the congregation would lift up a sorrowful, bitter cry over him.

But, I tell you, it is likely that not just one but many will remember this sermon while they are in hell. It would be surprising if some who are now present here were not in hell in a very short while, even before this year is over. I would not be amazed if some people now sitting here in this service in good health, content and secure, were there before tomorrow morning. Those of you who live and stay out of hell longer than others will surely be there before long! Your damnation is not sleeping; it will come swiftly and, most likely, very suddenly upon many of you.

You have good reason to wonder why you are not in hell already. I am sure that you have seen or known people who deserved hell no more than you, and who seemed as likely to remain alive as you. But now they are beyond hope; they are crying in extreme misery and complete despair. But, here you are in the land of the living and in the house of God, and you have an opportunity to obtain salvation. What would those poor, damned, hopeless souls not give for the opportunity you now have?

Now you have an extraordinary opportunity. This day Christ has thrown the door of mercy wide open and stands calling and crying with a loud voice to poor sinners. Many are flocking to Him and pressing into His kingdom. They are coming daily from the east and the west, from the north and the south. Many who until very recently, were in the same miserable condition that you are in, now are happy, their hearts filled with love for Him who has loved them and washed them from their sins in His own blood. They are rejoicing in hope of the glory of God. How terrible it would be to be left behind in such a day, to see others feasting while you are grieving and perishing! How awful it would be to see so many people rejoicing and singing with joy from their hearts while you can do nothing but mourn and feel sorrow in your heart, and cry because your spirit is so afflicted! How can you rest for one moment if you are now in that condition?

Are not your souls as valuable as the souls of the people at Suffield, where they are flocking every day to Christ? Are there not many here who have lived long in this world, but still are not born again? They are aliens of the commonwealth of Israel. All they have done for themselves since they were born is store up wrath for the coming day. Older men, you especially are in extreme danger. The guilt and hardness of your hearts are extremely great. Have you not noticed how often people of your years are passed over and left behind during this present wonderful time of God's mercy? You need to consider yourselves and thoroughly awaken out of your sleep. You cannot bear the fierceness of the infinite God.

As for you young men and young women, will you neglect this precious time you are now enjoying, when so many others your age are renouncing their youthful sins and flocking to Christ? You especially have an extraordinary opportunity. But if you neglect it, you will soon be like the other young people who spent all their precious days of youth in sin and have now gone to that dreadful place, full of blindness and hardness.

As for you children who are unconverted, do you not know that you are going to hell to bear the dreadful wrath of God, who is now angry with you every day and every night? Will you be content to be the children of the Devil when so many other children in the land are being converted and becoming the holy and happy children of the King of kings?

Now let everyone who is still without Christ and hanging over the pit of hell—whether old men or women, middle-aged people, young people or children—answer to the loud calls of God's Word and providence. This acceptable year of the Lord, a time of such great blessing to some, will surely be a day of remarkable vengeance to others. People's hearts become hard and their guilt increases if they neglect their souls in such a day as this. Never was there such danger of people being given to hardness of heart and blindness of mind.

God now seems to be quickly gathering in His elect in all parts of the land, and probably the majority of adults who will ever be saved will be brought in shortly. It will be like the great outpouring of the Spirit upon the Jews in the days of the apostles: the elect will obtain salvation, and the rest will be blinded. If the latter is true of you, you will eternally curse this day, as well as the day you were born. You have seen this great outpouring of God's Spirit but will wish you had died and gone to hell before you had seen it.

Now especially, as in the days of John the Baptist, the ax is laid at the roots of the trees so that every tree that does not bring forth good fruit will be cut down and cast into the fire.

Therefore, let everyone who is without Christ now wake up and flee from the wrath to come. The wrath of Almighty God is now, without a doubt, hanging over a great part of this congregation. Let everyone flee from Sodom, "Escape for your life! Do not look behind you nor stay anywhere in the plain. Escape to the mountains, lest you be destroyed" (Genesis 19:17).

Publisher's Postscript:
The Way of Life

WHEN JONATHAN EDWARDS first preached his now famous sermon on July 8, 1741, the response was amazing. The congregation in Enfield, Connecticut, where Edwards was a guest preacher, was filled with cries, shrieks, and moaning as people called out, asking how they could be saved. Edwards's passionate warning had convinced them that they were desperately close to being thrown into the endless torment of hell.

Perhaps as you have read this sermon you too have come to the alarming conviction that God's anger is directed at you. The Creator of the universe has designed you to love, worship, and obey Him, but you have devoted your energies to other things. God has not been very important in your life, and His truth revealed in the Bible has not meant much to you. But now you realize that you are on the wrong side of God, and nothing in this world—not your health or outward goodness or talents or even religious experiences—can spare you from the divine wrath you deserve.

Is there hope for you? Can sinners in the hands of an angry God become His forgiven children welcomed into the arms of their merciful heavenly Father?

The Bible's answer is a resounding *yes!* "For God so loved the world that He gave His only begotten Son, that whoever believes in Him should not perish but have everlasting life" (John 3:16). God has provided a way for sinners to have a new life—now and for eternity—instead of the eternal ruin Edwards has described. How can this new life be yours?

1. *Confess that you have a problem.* It is no exaggeration to say that you deserve the wrath of God you have just read about. "There is none righteous, no, not one" (Romans 3:10), Scripture says. "All have sinned and fall short of the glory of God" (Romans 3:23), and that includes you. But confessing this dreadful truth is the first step toward receiving the great news of salvation. "The wages of sin is death, but the gift of God is eternal life in Christ Jesus our Lord" (Romans 6:23).

2. *Acknowledge that God has the solution.* Though there is nothing you can do to win God's favor or pay for your sins, God sent His own Son, Jesus Christ, into the world to do for sinners what they could not do for themselves. The Son of God became man to live a perfect life and pay for the sins of others by His death on the cross. "God demonstrates His own love toward us, in that while we were still sinners, Christ died for us" (Romans 5:8). Not only did He die, but He also rose from the dead and now lives, ruling and reigning in heaven. Jesus "was raised to life for our justification" (Romans 4:25).

In other words, the same God who takes sin seriously enough to punish sinners in hell, has provided the way for us to be forgiven through His Son. And that way was Jesus Himself taking the place of sinners in the hands of an angry God.

3. *Turn from sin and trust Jesus.* You are faced with a choice. Your sins will be punished by a just God. The question is whether *you* will bear that eternal torment in hell or you will depend entirely on *Jesus'* shed blood as payment for your sin. Put your faith in Jesus Christ as your Savior and Lord. In other words, renouncing your sinful desires, believe that Jesus' death in your place has fully paid for your sin and His resurrection gives you a brand-new life. "If you confess with your mouth, 'Jesus is Lord,' and believe in your heart that God raised him from the dead, you will be saved" (Romans 10:9 NIV). By trusting in Him, you will have

- *a new record*—you will be pronounced not guilty, but righteous,
- *a new Master*—the Lord Jesus, not Satan or self,
- *new strength*—the spiritual freedom and power to grow in loving loyalty to Him.

4. *Live for God in reliance on Him.* Thankful for His past grace and trusting His future grace, live each day in glad fellowship with God, eager to learn more about Him, obey Him, and share the good news of Jesus with others who do not yet know Him. Go to God often in prayer, confident now that He loves and welcomes you. Read the Bible daily. And become a part of a church that believes the Bible as God's infallible Word, a church that will train and encourage you to serve Him.

"I [urge] you therefore, brethren, by the mercies of God, that you present your bodies a living sacrifice, holy, acceptable to God, which is your reasonable service. And do not be conformed to this world, but be transformed by the renewing of your mind, that you may prove what is that good and acceptable and perfect will of God." (Romans 12:1–2)

Why remain under the sentence of an angry God when the Lord Himself has offered terms of forgiveness and the privilege of living under His grace? Confess your sinfulness to God now. Let go of any pretense of your own "righteousness." Trust only in Jesus, who lived, died, and was raised to conquer sin and death. Ask God to open your blind eyes to your need for Him and to change your heart so that you will love Him for the great God He is. Tell Him you want to live for Him. And ask Him for forgiveness and a new life through His Son, Jesus Christ. God will answer your prayer, and you will know Him—now and for eternity—to be your marvelous heavenly Father.